THIS WALKER BOOK BELONGS TO:

_____

_____

_____

For Andy, Rob and Nick
with all my love
M.S.

For Mick with love
B.G.

First published 2000 by Walker Books Ltd
87 Vauxhall Walk, London SE11 5HJ

This edition published 2003

4 6 8 10 9 7

Text © 2000 Maddie Stewart
Illustrations © 2000 Brita Granström

Printed in China

British Library Cataloguing in Publication Data:
a catalogue record for this book
is available from the British Library

ISBN 978-0-7445-9806-3

www.walkerbooks.co.uk

Clever Daddy

Maddie Stewart

illustrated by
Brita Granström

WALKER BOOKS
AND SUBSIDIARIES
LONDON • BOSTON • SYDNEY • AUCKLAND

My daddy's very clever,
He's a very clever man,
He does all sorts of clever things
Like clever daddies can.

He can *swirl* me,
He can *twirl* me,
He can swing me
Round and round.

He can hold me high
And fly me,
He can swoosh me
To the ground.

He can sit me on his tummy,
He can bump me up and down,
He can make me laugh, he's funny –
My daddy is a clown.

My daddy's very clever,
He's as clever as can be,
He can build enormous towers,
Much taller ones than me.

He can be a lion
And jump out from behind,
He can be a spider,
The tickly wickly kind.

He can wash me,
Splish, splash, splosh me!
He can make my bathtime fun,
With lots of floaty boaty things
And bubbles on my tum.

He can put me on his shoulders
And even on his head,
He can chase me,
He can catch me,
He can flop me on the bed.

But now he's getting tired,
Clever daddies need to rest,
So we read a bedtime story,
The one I like the best.

He hugs me and he cuddles me
And tucks me up with Ted.
"Night night, Daddy."
"Night night, sleepy-head!"

WALKER BOOKS is the world's leading
independent publisher of children's books.
Working with the best authors and illustrators
we create books for all ages, from babies
to teenagers – books your child will
grow up with and always remember. So…

FOR THE BEST CHILDREN'S BOOKS,
LOOK FOR THE BEAR